A MESSAGE TO PARENTS

It is of vital importance for adults to read good books to young children in order to aid their psychological and intellectual development. As well as stimulating the child's imagination, it creates a positive relationship between adult and child. Reading aloud will also help children to increase their basic vocabulary and encourage them to begin reading alone. Brown Watson has published this series of books with these aims in mind. By collecting this inexpensive library, adults and children can share hours of pleasurable reading.

Printed in the E.C.

The Little Christmas Tree

Text by Maureen Spurgeon
Illustrated by Stephen Holmes

Brown Watson
ENGLAND

ONCE, on a hill above a town, there was a little Christmas tree. So many big trees grew all around, there was no room for the little tree to spread its roots, so it hardly grew at all. Nobody even knew that the tiny little Christmas tree was even there.

As Christmas time drew near, the little tree always felt so unhappy. He could see people looking at all the other trees and hear the children laughing and talking to each other.

"Ooh, look at that lovely big Christmas tree!"
"We can hang lots of presents on those strong branches!"
"This Christmas tree is so nice and tall!"

"Choose me!" thought the little Christmas tree. "Please choose me!" But nobody did. Then, one cold winter's night, something happened. Quite suddenly, a strong wind began to blow

The wind howled down all the chimneys, blew under all the doors and rattled all the windows. And it whistled through the branches of all the trees, tugging hard at the roots.

The little Christmas tree held on for as long as he could. But then a sudden gust of wind blew hard against the bottom branches and he felt himself being lifted high into the air!

"Whoo-Whoo!" whistled the wind, blowing harder than ever. Only one person saw the little Christmas tree whirling and twirling about on that cold, snowy night.

Gradually, the wind died down, as more big, white snowflakes fell from the sky. The little Christmas tree felt himself falling, falling, until he came to rest on a bed of snow.

"About time, too!" came a voice. And a figure in a red cloak and big boots picked up the little Christmas tree. "You always wanted to be a proper Christmas tree, didn't you?"

Little by little, the sky became lighter and a pale sun shone down. "Hey, here's the Christmas tree we wanted!" someone shouted. "Mum said Santa would bring it, Jason!"

"Let's take it indoors," came a boy's voice, "then we'll find a big flower pot or something and fill it with earth. We'll soon have this looking like a real Christmas tree!"

"I'm glad it's a little Christmas tree!" said Anna. "Big trees need lots of decorations!"
"And it's tall enough for me to reach the top branch!" laughed Jason. "I like it!"

They worked hard all morning, cutting out paper stars, making balls of silver foil and hanging things on all the branches. The little Christmas tree loved every minute!

There were lots of games and parties and fun around the little Christmas tree! Someone caught their sleeve on a branch and a piece broke off. But the little Christmas tree tried not to mind.

"Our poor tree!" said Anna.
"All its little green needles are beginning to fall off."
"That always happens," said someone else. "Christmas trees don't last long indoors!"

By the time Christmas was over, the little Christmas tree was very worried. "We'll put the decorations in the cupboard ready for next year!" said Mum. "Any rubbish for the dustmen?"

"What about the Christmas tree?" asked Jason. "We can't put that in the cupboard."

"No," said Mum, lifting the Christmas tree out of its flower pot. "It will have to go outside."

The poor little Christmas tree trembled so much that a whole shower of green needles fell to the ground. He was taken outside and set down by a cold wall, waiting for the dustmen.

After a while, the little tree was lifted up again – but he hardly cared. All he had ever wanted was to be a real Christmas tree. He had never been so unhappy.

He began to dream that he could hear birds singing, just as they did when he had been with the other trees on the hillside. He thought he heard a voice, sounding just like Jason.

"Look at the birds! They're eating all the food we've put round our tree!" The little Christmas tree looked down at his new, green branches, with the birds darting in and out.

"That little tree has certainly brightened up our back yard!" said Mum.

"YOU always said nothing would grow, because we don't get much sunshine!" said Jason.

"But we really don't WANT our Christmas tree to grow!" said Anna. And all through the months that followed, the birds would come and perch on the tree, chirping and singing.

As the days grew shorter, the time came for the birds to fly away to warmer lands. But the little Christmas tree did not mind. Soon, he knew, winter would come once again.